FOR THE MOTHER
OF THE GROOM

FOR THE MOTHER
OF THE GROOM

The Groom's Mother

Mary Martin

To order additional copies of this book, contact:
Xlibris Corporation
1-888-795-4274
www.Xlibris.com
Orders@Xlibris.com
16309

CONTENTS

FOR THE MOTHER
OF THE GROOM

This book is written **especially** for the **Mother** of the **Groom**. Whether you are the first time Mother of the Groom or not, this will guide you through the best of times and the worst of times.

ACKNOWLEDGEMENTS

This book would not be complete
If I failed to acknowledge
And eternally thank
The people who
Through their take on the world
And their love
Helped make it possible:
Mike, Sr.,
Matt,
Mike, Jr.,
Thomas,
Dolly,
Janet,
Anne,
Susan,
Mary,
Anna Marie,
And Julie.

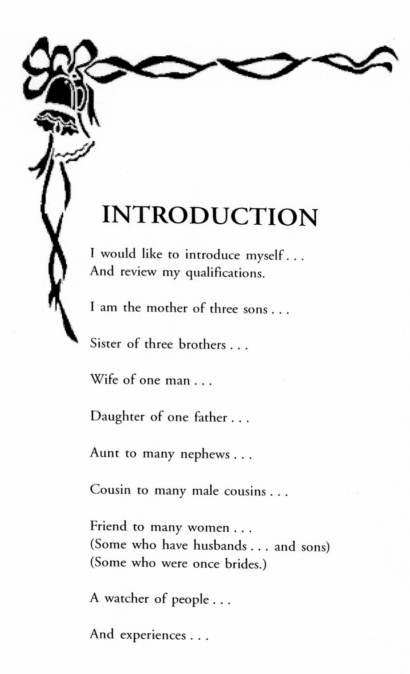

INTRODUCTION

I would like to introduce myself...
And review my qualifications.

I am the mother of three sons...

Sister of three brothers...

Wife of one man...

Daughter of one father...

Aunt to many nephews...

Cousin to many male cousins...

Friend to many women...
(Some who have husbands... and sons)
(Some who were once brides.)

A watcher of people...

And experiences...

DISCLAIMER

I have made some assumptions in this book.

They may not always be right . . .

But as you will learn,

It is not my fault.

THEY TELL YOU,
"YOU HAVE A SON!!!"

Awhile ago,

When you were much younger,

You fell in love . . .

Anyway, you know your own story

And can fill in the blanks.

Somewhere along the way

You were informed that you were having a baby.

Several months later . . .

THEY TELL YOU,
"YOU HAVE A SON!!!"

During a sweeter time,

When sex of your baby,

Was not known ahead of time . . .

You gave birth to a . . . *SON!*

SONS

When they handed you your son . . .

No one told you . . .

That you would fall hopelessly in love . . .

With this tiny needy person . . .

And that it would last a lifetime.

SONS

If someone did tell you,

You probably didn't listen.

And you couldn't possibly know . . .

That he would have the power . . .

To make you blissfully happy . . .

~ Or ~

Break your heart . . .

With hardly a thought . . .

At his very whim . . .

SONS

You were still looking at

That beautiful little face . . .

Knowing exactly where he was . . .

And whom he was with . . .

Usually, blissfully, *YOU!!!*

Those were the good old days.

SONS CONTINUED

As the years have gone by . . .

You have become stronger . . .

Stars have been knocked out of your eyes.

There have been hills . . .

And valleys,

Somedays . . .

Even you are sick of his antics.

But the love . . .

And the passion for his happiness . . .

Still runs deep in your heart.

SONS CONTINUED

When he was about two years old . . .

You tried to teach him how to share . . .

Sharing has never been an easy task to master . . .

For anyone . . .

Especially when they had no desire to share . . .

~ Or ~

Possibly give . . .

I sincerely hope that you remember the lessons . . .

You tried to teach . . .

You will need them now . . .

SONS CONTINUED

You are now faced with your biggest challenge . . .

And act of love . . .

Even though you are comfortable as . . .

The Mother of a son . . .

What Happens next . . .

It is not your fault.

The rules change!!!

You are now beginning your journey as the . . .

Mother of the Groom.

BEWARE!

This is a journey filled . . .

With traps and hazards.

I hope this book . . .

Will help guide you through a . . .

Safe . . .

Hopefully happy . . .

. . . Journey.

Good luck . . .

There will be days when you will need it.

FAMILY

Not only do I have brothers,

I also have a sister.

My sister . . .

Who has two daughters . . .

Loves her daughters . . .

Possibly, probably as passionately . . .

As I love my sons.

FAMILY

Sometimes . . .

When our children would be playing,

She would look over at them and say,

"I hope you are lucky enough

To have a daughter someday.

FAMILY

~ Or ~

Else . . .

You better enjoy these boys . . .

Now . . .

While they are yours.

Because you know that

Once

They get married . . .

FAMILY

Gasp!!!

The mother of the bride becomes the
MOTHER . . .

And the Mother of the groom becomes the
Mother-in-law!!!"

FAMILY

She said this several times over the years

And said it like it was a well known . . .

FACT!!!

As time went on,

I am sad to say . . .

That now . . .

I believe her.

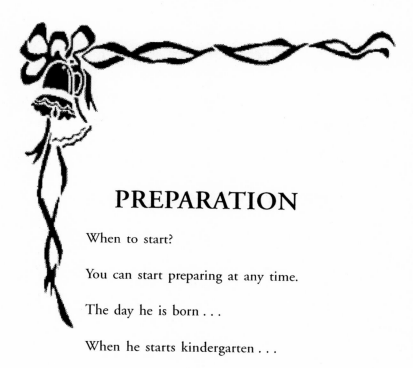

PREPARATION

When to start?

You can start preparing at any time.

The day he is born . . .

When he starts kindergarten . . .

PREPARATION

Even later . . .

It doesn't matter . . .

You can start early . . .

Hopefully make him husband worthy.

Teach him to cook . . .

And wash . . .

And fold . . .

PREPARATION

It doesn't matter . . .

You won't get extra credit for this . . .

So it is solely your choice.

If your son is already engaged . . .

You are already a little behind . . .

You can easily catch up.

THE WEDDING ANNOUNCEMENT

Your son is dating a girl . . .

A woman . . .

You may . . .

~ Or ~

May not like her . . .

It doesn't really matter.

THE WEDDING ANNOUNCEMENT

You may know the girlfriend . . .

But now she is the bride.

THE WEDDING ANNOUNCEMENT

You will get to know each other better . . .

Especially if there is a big wedding.

THE WEDDING ANNOUNCEMENT

You may

~ Or ~

May not

Be aware that this announcement is coming.

If your son is of a certain age . . .

Anywhere over the age of consent . . .

Whatever that is . . .

Be prepared!

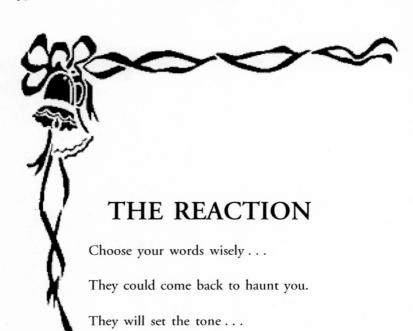

THE REACTION

Choose your words wisely . . .

They could come back to haunt you.

They will set the tone . . .

Be very . . . very careful!!!

Say something like,

"This is so special!"

~ Or ~

"Congratulations!!!"

THE REACTION

Do not say,

"Oh NO!!!"

~ Or ~

"WHAT, you've got to be kidding???"

THE REACTION

Be or act happy . . .

Listen carefully.

Don't offer any advice . . .

~ Or ~

Suggestions.

THE REACTION

Be or act happy!!!

Breathe . . .

But not too deeply . . .

They'll notice!!!

. . . This is only the beginning.

BE POSITIVE

You may be very lucky . . .

The ring may have been bought and paid for . . .

They may have saved money . . .

Enough to pay for the wedding

Enough to buy the house!!!

Bless them!!!

BE POSITIVE

You may not be as lucky.

They may be expecting.

Hardly have carfare to get to work . . . if they have jobs.

They may want a wedding fit for royalty.

THEY MAY WANT TO MOVE IN WITH YOU!!!

BE POSITIVE

You may fall somewhere in the middle . . .

A girl you like,

But still some concerns . . .

This book is helpful no matter what the circumstances.

LISTEN

Everybody has a story . . .

You were young once . . .

LISTEN

Some brides know exactly

What they want their wedding to be.

After all,

Some have dreamed about it all their lives.

Some have mothers . . .

Mothers who have also dreamed about it all their lives.

LISTEN SOME MORE

Some brides have themes . . .

~ Or ~

Visions . . .

Cinderella . . .

Horse carriages . . .

Hot air balloons . . .

Who knows what.

They may be her visions . . .

LISTEN SOME MORE

~ Or ~

Their visions.

(Their being the bride and your son . . . her groom . . .

~ Or ~

Their being the bride and her Mother . . .)

LISTEN SOME MORE

They may not be your visions . . .

But you are not the bride . . .

Alas . . .

You . . .

Are the Mother of the Groom.

LISTEN SOME MORE

They are not interested in your visions . . .

No matter what they say . . .

Know this to be a true!!!

They are not interested in your visions!!!

LISTENING IS
A GOOD THING

Some brides come from small families . . .

Some brides want a small intimate wedding . . .

LISTENING IS A GOOD THING

You may have 200 close relatives . . .

And friends . . .

~ Or ~

Vice versa . . .

There are a lot of variables.

LISTEN CLOSELY

Things change quickly . . .

They definitely may want something . . .

And after pricing it $$$

They may still want it . . .

~ Or ~

Maybe not.

If you are not writing the check . . .

It is none of your business!!!

LISTEN CAREFULLY

If they are heading in a direction . . .

That you are not thrilled with . . .

But doesn't offend you . . .

Let it go!!!

LISTEN AND LEARN

For Instance . . .

If they give you the number of people you can invite . . .

And you want to just **JUMP** off the roof . . .

Because you want to invite more . . .

Stay calm!!!

LISTEN AND LEARN

Pick your issues carefully . . .

Pause . . .

Take a breath . . .

Again . . .

Not too deep . . .

They will notice!

LISTEN AND LEARN

They would think of it as a sigh of frustration . . .

They may be right . . .

But we can't allow that to happen.

Listen and learn.

LISTEN AND BE THOUGHTFUL

Take another breath . . .

Then ask . . .

Can the room accommodate a few more people?

LISTEN AND BE THOUGHTFUL

If so,

Would you be able to invite a few more guests???

And of course . . .

You would insist on paying for your additional guests.

LISTEN AND BE SMART

If they agree . . .

Great!

LISTEN AND BE SMART

If they look distressed . . .

If they sigh . . .

Tell them the number they gave was fine . . .

And work with it.

End of story.

So your Aunt whatever her name is won't speak to you . . .

We'll deal with that later.

Smile, be smart.

It is not your fault!!!

LISTEN, CONTINUED . . .

Handle the number they gave you . . .

As best as you can . . . .

LISTEN, CONTINUED . . .

You can always call anyone you think will be hurt . . .

Tell them you son is getting married . . .

And you would love to invite them . . .

You always planned on inviting them to your sons

Wedding . . .

But the bride's family is handling everything!!!

You were given only a small number of invitations!!!

Of course you offered to pay for more . . .

But they said where they are getting married can

Accommodate only a small number . . .

And they said no!!!

LISTEN, CONTINUED . . .

People will be kind to you . . .

They will understand . . .

It is not your fault . . .

You are the Mother of the Groom.

When in doubt . . .

Put the onus on the bride . . .

And her family!

After all, you are only the Mother of the Groom . . .

Nothing is your **fault!**

CONTROL

There will be few things that you will have control over . . .

Accept this . . .

As they make plans . . .

They may or may not include you . . .

CONTROL

You are strong . . .

You will set the tone . . .

If you are pleasant . . .

Non-judgmental . . .

They may share more . . .

If you look at them at times . . .

Like they are too stupid to live . . .

Well . . .

They will include you less . . .

CONTROL

If you act too detached . . .

They will not like that either . . .

If you think this is a trap . . .

It is . . .

CONTROL

There are two expressions that you should practice.

One is . . .

'What a great idea!'

The other is . . .

'Hmmm, I would never have thought of that!'

These expressions will work in all situations.

CONTROL CONTINUED

For instance . . .

The bride and groom share all their plans with you . . .

And they are perfect.

You say, "What a great idea."

CONTROL CONTINUED

~ Or ~

They come to you . . .

With less-than-perfect plans,

But not terrible . . .

You say the same thing.

CONTROL CONTINUED

~ Or ~

They come to you . . .

With the most ridiculous plans you ever heard . . .

But they are not final . . .

And may get better.

Instead of saying 'Are you insane',

You say, "Hmmm I would never have thought of that."

CONTROL CONTINUED

Say it in a tone that is mild . . .

And possibly thoughtful . . .

In your mind

You can add, "Because it is stupid!"

Breathe . . . But not too deeply . . .

They are watching!!!

CONTROL CONTINUED

If they are missing the boat on something . . .

Or there is something . . .

That is important to you . . .

That you would like . . .

This something has a monetary value . . .

Here is what to do . . . .

CONTROL CONTINUED

Pick a good time . . .

Suggest to the bride and groom whatever it is . . .

Then add that you would like to pay for it . . .

If they go for it, great!!!

If they don't . . .

CONTROL CONTINUED

You are allowed to ask or suggest two more times only . . .

If they don't go for it let it go . . .

It is not worth it . . .

Watch their body language . . .

Before you decide to ask the second time . . .

If you have questions limit them to one a week . . .

Don't be pushy, don't badger them . . .

It is not worth the stress . . . and they will hate you!!!

CONTROL CONTINUED

You definitely

Don't want to get the reputation of being interfering!!!

~ Or ~

Worse . . .

Have the bride roll her eyes . . .

Every time your son mentions your name!!!

CONTROL CONTINUED

You do have control over three things.

First, the wedding shower gift.

Follow your family traditions.

You may be invited to more then one.

Whatever you do and buy,

Do it with joy in your heart.

If someone in your family decides to have a shower,

Let people know what your son likes,

What his hobbies are.

CONTROL CONTINUED

For instance,

My cousin Mike was getting married . . .

And we really didn't know his intended very well.

We knew that Mike liked to camp.

My sister, mother and I pooled our money

We gave him a great ice chest

And other camping things.

CONTROL CONTINUED

When the bride opened the gifts

She happily said, "Mike will love these gifts . . .

And I do too!"

We came to love his wife,

And are delighted to have

Such a wonderful addition to our family.

CONTROL CONTINUES

Second, (and most important) the dress!

No, not the brides dress!!!

Your dress!!!

This **is** probably the only real thing . . .

That you have control over.

You may have months . . . even a year to pick out your
dress.

CONTROL CONTINUES

Take your time . . .

Save if you have to . . .

You really must look great at your son's wedding!!!

Have fun looking for it . . .

Go everywhere!!!

Bring friends or a relative . . .

Shop in stores you've never been in . . .

CONTROL CONTINUES

Have your colors done . . .

Work out . . . .

Tradition suggests . . .

You ask the bride's mother what color she is wearing . . .

Find out what color the bridal party's wearing as well . . .

Find a dress that complements these colors . . . if you want.

Remember . . .

There will be photographs!!!

CONTROL IS GOOD

Indulge yourself!

The only person . . .

Who should look better than you.

Maybe . . .

Possibly . . .

Is . . .

The bride!!!

INVITATIONS

Simple, or so you thought . . .

They could be traditional . . .

Parchment stock with an elegant script font.

They could be clever . . .

They could be original . . .

They could be loud and large . . .

Pray for good taste . . .

And remember . . .

If they are loud with doves and rings in primary
colors . . .

It is not your fault!!!

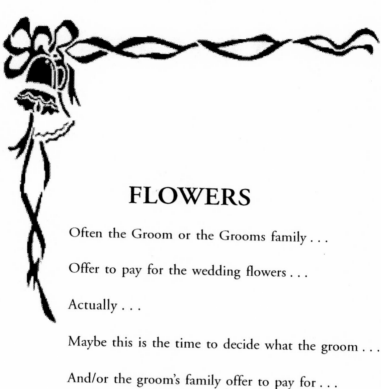

FLOWERS

Often the Groom or the Grooms family . . .

Offer to pay for the wedding flowers . . .

Actually . . .

Maybe this is the time to decide what the groom . . .

And/or the groom's family offer to pay for . . .

Flowers seem to be a gift to the bride . . .

It is a nice thing for the groom to provide . . .

And for all the important women in the groom's life . . .

Mothers . . . Grandmothers . . . God Mothers . . .
    Bridal Party . . .

All get flowers . . .

DECISIONS

Then there are the rings . . .

Honeymoon . . .

A menu of things that the groom . . .

~ Or ~

His family can offer to pay for . . .

Go out and buy an etiquette book . . .

DECISIONS

There are so many variables when it comes to this . . .

Religion . . .

Tradition . . .

Etc . . .

You have two answers when it comes to financial

Requests . . .

YES . . . NO . . . I have no opinion on this, you are on your own!!!

THE REHEARSAL DINNER

The third thing that you have some control over is the rehearsal dinner . . .

This is your party.

You can do yourself . . .

And your son proud!!!

Have it at a restaurant . . .

THE REHEARSAL DINNER

~ Or ~

In your home . . .

~ Or ~

Anywhere you please . . .

Have a ball planning it . . .

Make it elegant . . .

~ Or ~

Casual . . .

THE REHEARSAL DINNER

Have a theme if you want!!!

Serve his favorite food . . .

~ Or ~

Yours!!!

Whatever you do . . .

Enjoy planning it . . .

Spend a little . . .

THE REHEARSAL DINNER

Spend a lot . . .

Be kind to yourself . . .

Your son . . .

And his bride . . .

.

This is where you step up to the plate . . .

And shine!!!

THE REHEARSAL DINNER

The wedding party . . .

Bride and groom . . .

Family . . .

Out of town family . . .

The Priest, Minister, Justice of the Peace, Rabbi

~ Or ~

Whoever will officiate the ceremony . . .

Are all invited . . . All will enjoy the dinner

All will eat and drink and have a great time.

THE REHEARSAL DINNER

This is the celebration before the wedding.

So celebrate!!! They will know that you are the host.

Don't forget to look great . . . Pictures again!!!

(I have a great cheese ball recipe to share with you!)

THE WEDDING DAY!

Finally!!!

It's here . . .

You will have a daughter-in-law . . .

THE WEDDING DAY!

Things have gone wonderfully . . .

THE WEDDING DAY!

~ Or ~

Things have gone pretty well . . .

THE WEDDING DAY

~ Or ~

Things have just . . .

Gone.

THE WEDDING DAY, CONTINUED

You are joyous!!!

THE WEDDING DAY CONTINUED

~ Or ~

You are happy . . .

THE WEDDING DAY CONTINUED

~ Or ~

You just are . . .

THE WEDDING DAY CONTINUED

No matter what . . .

You look great!!!

You love your son . . .

Hopefully,

You love his bride . . .

Very soon to be wife.

THE WEDDING DAY
CONTINUED

~ Or ~

You will come to love her . . .

THE WEDDING DAY CONTINUED

~ Or ~

You question his taste in women . . .

But will think of this on *another day!!!*

Not now.

THE WEDDING CEREMONY

The ceremony is lovely . . .

Whether it is a religious ceremony . . .

~ Or ~

A civil one . . .

They have pledged their love . . .

Maybe, in front of God . . .

Definitely in front of witnesses.

Whether the ceremony takes place in a church . . .

THE WEDDING CEREMONY

A Temple,
An auditorium,
A house,
A home,
A hill,
~ Or ~
A hotel,

These are things that you . . .

The Mother of the Groom can't decide . . .

THE WEDDING CEREMONY

Just close your eyes . . .

Listen to the words that are spoken . . . .

They have pledged their love to each other . . .

You can quietly pledge your love and support . . .

You made it this far!

THE RECEPTION

The reception can take place any place . . .
A reception hall,
A house,
A back yard,
A fire hall,
A hotel,
A restaurant,
A park,
A Caribbean Beach
A church hall . . .

Wherever it is . . .

You are now at the reception.

THE RECEPTION

It is wonderful!!!

Everything you have ever dreamed of for him!

The music is great.

Everyone is dancing.

You are so proud . . .

Of him . . .

For him . . .

Of her.

When everyone compliments you,

You just smile and say,

"Thank You."

THE RECEPTION

~ Or ~

You are at the reception . . .

And it is not what you would have planned . . .

But it is nice.

He is happy.

When people compliment you . . .

You just smile and say,

"I can't take any credit . . .

They did it all.

I hope you enjoy yourself."

THE RECEPTION

~ Or ~

You are at the reception.

It is awful!!!

Your worst nightmare.

When guests say anything . . .

Just smile and whisper . . .

"The bride's family made all the arrangements!"

They will know that you are the Mother of the Groom.

Nothing is your fault!

THE DANCE

No, not the first dance,

Not the 'Daddy's little girl dance.'

It's the Groom will dance with his Mother dance!

THE DANCE

Now this gets interesting!!!

Does the groom pick out the song???

Or, do you???

Of course it was decided long before this point,

But I have heard it done both ways.

I like the groom to surprise his Mother with his choice . . .

But it is not up to me.

However, I can make some suggestions,

Because this is my book.

THE DANCE

The song can be happy . . .

~ Or ~

A tearjerker . . .

Sentimental . . .

~ Or ~

Funny . . .

THE DANCE

You can be a good dancer . . .

~ Or ~

Not . . .

But remember . . .

Everyone will be watching!!!

More Pictures

And yes . . .

Let's not forget the video!

THE DANCE

Here are a few suggestions:

Song For My Mama	Boys II Men
Just the way you are	Billy Joel
Our House	Madness
Oh How The Years Go By	Amy Grant
I'll Always Love My Mama	Temptations
What A Wonderful World	Louis Armstrong

There are so many to choose from,

Two that I would stay away from are:

Tell Mama,	Etta James
Shop Around,	Smokey Robinson
	And The Miracles

THE DANCE

You hold him in your arms . . .

One more time . . .

He is so beautiful . . .

He always was . . .

How wonderful for you . . .

That you are the Mother of the Groom . . .

I bet he whispers in your ear,

"I love you, Mom."

And then you realize . . .

Your work is done.

LATER THAT NIGHT . . .

The wedding is over . . .

You had the time of your life . . .

You are blissfully happy . . .

Except for the little tear in your eye . . .

Your son . . .

Your baby . . .

Is now a married man . . .

He has married the woman of his dreams . . .

And maybe yours too.

LATER THAT NIGHT . . .

You are satisfied because you took the high road.

You know in his heart he loves you . . .

And is proud of you . . .

He may even have said so!

You took the high road!!!

You have come to love your new daughter-in-law.

LATER THAT NIGHT

~ Or ~

The Wedding's over.

It's not what you would have planned . . .

But you had fun.

The bride . . .

Now wife . . .

And you are still speaking.

Success!!!

LATER THAT NIGHT

~ Or ~

The wedding is over.

Thank goodness . . .

It was pretty awful . . .

You lived through it . . .

Everyone is still speaking . . .

Now it is time to take that deep breath!!!

(And always remember . . .
And never forget.
He can have more than one wife . . .
But only one Mother...)

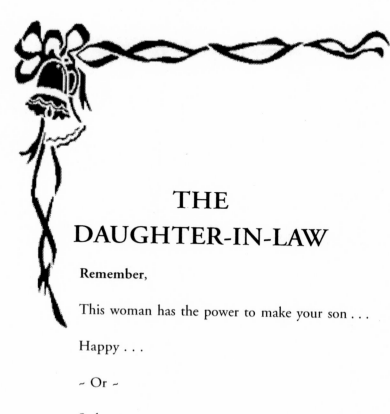

THE DAUGHTER-IN-LAW

Remember,

This woman has the power to make your son . . .

Happy . . .

~ Or ~

Sad . . .

She can share a happy . . .

Satisfying life with him . . .

And even give you grandchildren!!!

If you are kind and loving . . .

This marriage may turn out to be the best ever!!!

THE
DAUGHTER-IN-LAW

And . . .

If their love overflows . . .

And includes you . . .

THE DAUGHTER-IN-LAW

Hopefully along the way . . .

The two of you made a silent pact . . .

As woman to woman . . .

To be kind to each other . . .

To respect each other . . .

To agree to disagree . . .

The best thing ever is that you were lucky enough to be . . .

The Mother of the Groom.

LOVE

Sometimes . . .

When things take on a life of it's own . . .

We forget the important things . . .

LOVE

Why we are here . . .

What we all want . . .

What makes life worthwhile . . .

I have hoped everyday . . .

Since my sons were born . . .

That they would find love.

And that they would be lucky enough . . .

To have that love returned.

If you are reading this book . . .

If you are buying the dress . . .

If you are planning the dinner . . .

I congratulate you.

LOVE

What a powerful woman you must be . . .

For having raised,

The man,

Who made you the Mother of the Groom.

You have raised a man who is lovable!!!

And husband worthy!!!

BEST WISHES

Best wishes to all mothers . . .

Especially the Mother's of sons.

Best wishes to all brides . . .

Be kind to the woman who raised the man

You fell in love with.

BLESSINGS

Mothers

God wove a web of loveliness

Of clouds and stars and birds

But made not anything at all

As beautiful as mother's words:

They are as fair

As blooms or air,

They shine like every star:

And I am rich who learn from her

How beautiful they are.

BLESSINGS

Marriage Blessing

May God be with you and bless you.

May you see your children's children

May you be poor in misfortune.

Rich in Blessing.

May you have nothing but happiness

From this day forward.

BLESSINGS

May your mornings bring you joy

And your evenings bring you peace.

May your troubles grow few

And your blessings increase.

May the saddest day of your future

Be no worse then the happiest day of your past.

May your hands be forever clasped in friendship

And your hearts joined forever in love.

BLESSINGS

Home

May your troubles be less,

And your blessings be more,

And nothing but happiness,

Come through your door.

May joy and peace surround you,

Contentment latch your door,

And happiness be with you now

And bless you ever more.

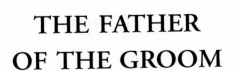

THE FATHER
OF THE GROOM

You may think . . .

That I have forgotten . . .

About the Father of the Groom.

I didn't.

I sleep every night . . .

Happily . . .

With the father of my potential grooms.

Like I said,

We all have our own stories.

One of the Fathers . . .

Will have to write his own book.

NO TAKE BACKS

I think somewhere during all this planning . . .

All this preparation . . .

That both the Mother of the Groom . . .

And the Mother of the Bride . . .

Remind both the bride and groom . . .

That there are no 'take backs' . . .

Marriage should not be taken lightly . . .

There are no fall back plans.

ANNIVERSARIES

Let's Be Positive!

1 Paper
2 Cotton
3 Leather
4 Books, fruit, flowers
5 Wood or clocks
6 Irons or Candy
7 Copper, bronze, brass
8 Electrical
9 Pottery
10 Tin or aluminum
11 Steel
12 Silk or Linen
13 Lace
14 Ivory
15 Crystal

ANNIVERSARIES

Congratulations if you ever need to reference this page!

20   China

25   Silver

30   Pearl

35   Jade or coral

40   Ruby

45   Sapphire

50   Gold

GUEST LISTS

Name   **Address**

RECIPE

Cheese Ball

1 Stick of Pepperoni Grated
2 Packages Philadelphia Cream Cheese
Paprika
Triscuit Crackers

Squish together the cream cheese
And pepperoni.
I f you are having a bad day,
Squish until you feel better.
If you are having a good day,
Take pleasure in a great cheese ball!
Roll into a ball.
Roll until covered with paprika.

Garnish and serve with crackers

Only the beginning!

Best wishes to all and to all a good life!

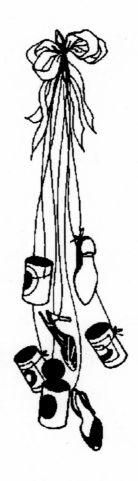

Printed in the United States
20743LVS00006B/27

9 781401 072575